ISBN 978-0-9781705-8-5

Interview used by the kind permission
of Jelaluddin Boru

http://www.shamcher.org

Alpha Glyph Publications Ltd.
http://alphaglyph.com

An Interview

with

Shamcher Bryn Beorse

Recorded by Jelaluddin Boru

From the Shamcher Archives

An Interview with Shamcher Bryn Beorse was recorded in the late 1970s, probably in 1978, by Jelaluddin Boru, in San Francisco, California. This interview gives an overview of Shamcher's views on a variety of topics, but in particular it was intended to become part of a book on obsession and the misunderstandings based on dependence on mediumship. However, like much of Shamcher's work, this interview defies specific categorization.

We are happy to make this transcription available to those who are interested in Shamcher's work and approach.

The Shamcher Archives have been collected and maintained by Carol Sill and Vakil Forest Shomer, with contributions from the friends, family and colleagues of Shamcher Bryn Beorse. Many of these archival documents relate to energy and economics, specifically OTEC and Giro-credit. Others focus on the mystical path of the sufis.

Find more on Shamcher's work at
http://shamcher.wordpress.com or www.shamcher.org.

Carol Sill, Vancouver, BC, 2007

AN INTERVIEW WITH SHAMCHER BRYN BEORSE

RECORDED BY JELALUDDIN BORU

RADICAL POLITICS

Jelaluddin: There are some people, all them radicals if you will, who believe that you can only change the world, and you don't need to change yourself.

Shamcher: Yes. They are a little bit further out of balance than most Sufis are, and that is fine, it is their task, and they may do a lot of good. But if they say they don't need to change themselves, they are wrong for whether they know it or not, they are still doing it. So many of them have come back entirely changed! For instance, how many people who in the '60s threw bombs and everything, have come back now with an entirely different attitude? And maybe they didn't think that they had changed themselves, but they have anyway.

Of course it is always wrong from an absolute point of view to use violence. You hit the wrong people.

I know of a case where a black killed a journalist who had been with them all the time. He had been fighting for the blacks and came down to see what happened. He was just another 'whitey' in this situation and got killed. And this kind of thing is just typical. When you throw a bomb at a house, how do you know who inside that structure will be killed? It may be the very people you want to protect and help. And the same goes for the police. They are paid by the community to do a certain work, and they don't have any choice. So to challenge them is wrong, you are challenging the wrong people!

Or take the case of a strike against a factory owner. He could be the best man in the world and really trying to help his workers, but the strike is against him instead of the thoughtless president, the more thoughtless cabinet members, the sometimes thoughtless scientists; the people who are really to blame, the greedy ones whose only thought is how they can enrich themselves.

It is this kind of confusion that makes violence totally unacceptable. Violence is never acceptable as a way of helping or promoting a good cause. And the people who use it are only acceptable as primitive extremists on an individual course, just like criminals are acceptable.

Inayat Khan was once approached by criminals, with guns, because they knew he was a holy man and they wanted him to perform a marriage for one of them. And he said, "O yes, of course. With pleasure I will come." And the criminals in great surprise put away their guns, and he went out there and married them and came back.

MEMORY AS A BALANCER

Jelaluddin: In a recent issue of *The Message,* Pir [Vilayat] talks about carrying a sense of memory from moment to moment. It seems that balance is like this. Rather than having one's interest burn up like a flame, and then losing all the impressions and lessons learned in the particular point of attention, would you say that an essential part of balance is continuity?

Shamcher: Right. On your path you should try to remember at least this life. And maybe more than that, all the way from the beginning. That's why I touched on the unbalance I had when I was younger, when I had to go on those mountain trips etc. I don't need that any longer, maybe because now the hills are so darn steep (hmmmn, is it because I don't need it, or the combination of these two things together?) But it is true, one should try one's best to remember all the lessons, and then it is easier to be in communication with all ages.

Jelaluddin: Perhaps it is best to say that there is no balance greater than the awareness that you are one with God, and once you realize this, no matter what happens, there is a sense of Beauty and Divinity in you.

Shamcher: Yes. That's very, very true, I couldn't improve upon it.

Jelaluddin: I think you said it.

Shamcher: Yes?

OBSESSION

Jelaluddin: Shamcher, I've been searching for the underlying similarity in the type of obsession we've talked about. The "obsession" of Inayat Khan's interest, contact with spirits of the other side, and the obsession that is preoccupation with certain ideas of the mind, and the obsession that is a process towards living with ego in balance. Somehow it is all caught up with the old idea from the *Gita* that deals with attachment to the fruits of one's labors.

Shamcher: Yes, Obsession only occurs when you are concerned with the fruits of your labor. There is an old piece of wisdom in both yogic and Sufi lore, and that is that you may be fond of your labor, you may do your labor for humanity, but if you think about the fruits and are concerned primarily with them then you are off the track, and for our purposes here you could say such a one was obsessed. For instance, you do certain things, and are overanxious with the result. "Will they understand me, will they go along, will I have no success at all?" Such thoughts make an obsession out of your work.

Jelaluddin: There seem to be two sides of dealing with this, On the one hand, the idea of struggle into self mastery, as suggested by the *Gita* quote: "O Arjuna, you can fight. " And the other approach which is to yield to one's impulses and "go with the flow. "

3

Shamcher: You give in to the flow, but this is perhaps not as simple as it sounds. Say there is a trend in our civilization right now to strive for more income. Civilization tells you that you are a bigger and better person the more you get. If you give in to this, you are not giving in to the flow, you are giving in to a quirk of civilization. There is a difference.

Congressmen, for instance, who feel that they must be privileged to increase their salaries in correspondence with inflation (which they are perhaps more responsible for than anyone else), they are giving in to the flow in a certain sense, but what flow? A flow of incorrect civilization. Giving in to the flow really means giving in to the flow that is the flow of the Universe, of the spirit. It is important to know which flow we are speaking of.

Like the way we give awards, titles, prizes. A person receives a Ph.D. or a Nobel prize. One rather wise head of a university once said: "I'd like to add a little note on everyone who gets their Ph.D. 'This man has strived hard to become a very narrow specialist in this field, so never listen to him in anything else. '" This is the correct way, this man was trying to listen to the real flow. Whereas the others, the ones who have such great respect because they are Ph.D.s or some other title of being a great scientist, may be giving in to another flow altogether different, and one quite unworthy.

TITLES

Jelaluddin: That leads right into the idea of titles: Masters, Pir-O-Murshids, etc.

Shamcher: Yes, even the religious and philosophical organizations seem to have sinned in this direction. Hazrat Inayat Khan, a "Pir-O-Murshid", once said; "When a title is given to a person, it doesn't mean he is more advanced or is in any way ahead of anyone else, it means that he is privileged to have extended to him the opportunity to see if someday he may arrive at the proper attitude of respect, gratitude and humbleness that goes with his being a Sufi.

Inayat Khan's second son, Hidayat, says that he remembers that his

4

father said, when he went to India the last time. "If I ever come back, I shall forget about the titles and the hierarchy and concentrate on the message." And some will say "Well, Hidayat was a child at the time and you can remember a child remembering something like that". But I was 29 years old at the time and I remember the same thing. Of course I was a child too. Am still a child for that matter.

I believe that among Sufis we have all kinds of people. Some are more sensitive than others, and some believe in the hierarchy as a means to help the pupil, and maybe in some instances that is good. Personally, I am against it. I don't think that it does any good, and I've always asked that no one use the title that I have been accorded in the Sufi effort [Murshid]. I certainly don't feel that I deserve any title.

Sometimes people say, "You must have respect and call Inayat Khan Pir-O-Murshid Inayat Khan. That's the last thing I want to call him. I've always felt that he is so much more than merely a Pir-O-Murshid. I have met many murshids and Pir-O-Murshids for whom I could have no respect whatever, and others whom I felt were very fine people. So you see that it has nothing to do with the title.

Jelaluddin: About Inayat Khan. Would you say that all of his grace and power then, came from his natural attunement with the grace of his message, a message born of the vibrations coming from us?

Shamcher: He once said: "I was sent to the West by my teacher to unite East and West with the music that you know; and I did that in the beginning. I played my music, and now I have come to hear the music of every living Soul and this is not merely uniting the geographical directions of east and west but any two apparently opposite units, uniting them through the harmony which I hear when I listen to the music from individuals." And by this he didn't think that these individuals were going to sing to him, but he heard something, he looked at the person and the vibrations that he felt was the music he heard. So in one sense he stopped his musical life, but really it was a continuance of the same thing: uniting east and west through the harmony of his music.

5

Harmony

Jelaluddin: Harmony is so much a part of the message. And mastery of the forces within us so much a part of mastering the outer conflict which tends to separate us from our fellow beings. Yet how often we know nothing about how to go about learning self-control. And because of this lack of knowledge a very good intention becomes distorted and our appetites become exaggerated, and then explode outwardly in a very dangerous manner later on. Do you have any practical methods to recommend for the control of appetites, for the balancing of obsession?

Shamcher: It is all very, very individual. When I was young I enjoyed fasting. I now know that is not the right way for everybody. I would fast for two or three weeks, eat nothing, and hardly even drink anything. Now, for some people that would be terrible. But I survived and even worked as usual and felt as strong. Sometimes I felt a little cooler.
The trouble was when I began eating again. The tendency is to eat too much. One should start with very little. An apple or a cracker, for if you eat too much you may destroy all the good effects of the fast. But the most important effect one gets from a fast is the feeling one starts to get about this body of yours.
WHO is really taking care of it?!

Mediums

Jelaluddin: I would like you to speak on mediums, as this book is essentially to spread Inayat Khan's last thoughts on obsession.

Shamcher: Among mediums there are many types. There is the type such as Eileen Garrett for example. A very developed spiritual person whose mediumicity was colored and directed by her soul. Or by her mind at least, and most mediums are not of this class. Most mediums are in touch with spirits and departed beings in a way that is not directed, and because of this the things which come from the other side can only mix them up.

It is because of this confusion that Inayat Khan used his last 4 hours to talk to us about mediums and obsession. And one of the things he said was, "The teacher never, never talks to a pupil through a medium. If he wants to reach a pupil he talks to them directly." He described in some detail the trouble he'd had in his life in dealing with mediums, and he said that they are not usually spiritually advanced people, they are merely people with a certain kind of gift, or which can be described as a gift or a handicap as you choose.

Anyway, the thing about most mediums is that they have no capacity of discrimination, and they believe in everything which comes from the other side. I have met so many people who say. "Oh, I have direct guidance from the other side!" Well, the other side is just as full of cheating and nonsense as this side, even more so.

And you know, after Inayat had warned us, after he had gone to the other side, four of his closest disciples, with high titles, came to Suresnes, and said, "I must tell you that I have been appointed to be the leader of the whole Sufi movement. I have been told by a medium." One of these was a Norwegian leader that I knew very well, and so I asked her if she didn't remember what Inayat had said. And she answered, "But the medium told me something that nobody else except Inayat Khan and myself knew, so it must be genuine!" There was no stopping her.

Jelaluddin: From your book *Man and the Mysterious Universe*, One time you use the phrase "the enemy within", which you define as "anything which prevents man from becoming master of his own destiny". Would you say that this is precisely what mediums are doing - interfering with capacities to become masters of ourselves, because they initiate us a habit of dependence upon them for our guidance?

Shamcher: That is so very true, I very much agree with you. I have seen, unfortunately, several Sufis who have gone to seek mediums and fortune tellers. Which of course prevents them from pursuing their own ability. And which, even worse, prevents them from thinking clearly. I have been seeing more and more of this. I had a good friend who finally left the whole Sufi movement because she became so dependent on that kind of impulse. It is strange, in a sense, because the whole of Sufi teaching is to develop the direct sides of the person himself.

An illustration of this is the farewell address of the Buddha:

Therefore, o Ananda, be a lamp unto yourself.
Rely on yourself and do not rely on external help,
Holding fast to the truth as a lamp.
Seek salvation alone in the truth.
and look not for assistance to anyone besides yourself!
And how, o Ananda, can a person be a lamp unto himself?
By holding fast unto the truth, holding to the truth as his lamp,
Seeking salvation alone in the truth
and not looking to anyone except himself.
And those, who either now, or after I am dead,
shall be a lamp unto themselves, looking only to themselves
and not relying an any external help,
it is they, Ananda, among my bhikkus,
who shall reach the topmost height.
As long as they are anxious to learn.

Today, Americans, and Europeans too, are too eager to run to a teacher in the sense of a guide, and not to even bother with investigating themselves. Today anyone can turn up and say, "I am a teacher" and he immediately has a following of thousands of people with lots of money to spare.

Jelaluddin: How does one go about this self-investigation?

Shamcher: The mind is a good instrument of discrimination, and as Inayat Khan says, "The mind and the heart are as two wheels of a carriage." We must utilize them both in a process that is balanced. An example is the story of the yoga aspirant. This one had such a keen mind developed that when a bird disturbed his meditation he was able to send up a flame of fury and the bird was burnt to a crisp. That is a mind without a heart. It is only when the mind and heart are in balance that one can go about the real process of self-investigation. Then you can develop the powers of the mind and direct them with the heart to the area that you want.

If you want to use the mind to understand yourself, then you express it as a desire of the heart. You say "Yes, I want understanding." But you do it gently, you don't ask in a fury, that's not the right way. Anything that your mind wants legitimately, that is, directed by the heart, and which it has a right to want, will come. Either this same second, or perhaps a week later, or even a thousand years later sometimes. You don't know when, but this doesn't mean you postpone it by saying, "Oh, it may not come for a thousand years." You simply say "I want it." Just say that.

Ego

Jelaluddin: I think that these Sufis, or other people, who have run to mediums, oracles, etc., are often doing so because of a basically good purpose of developing their intuition in such a way that they are in touch with the deeper significance of their lives, the one contained within their surface wants. And it is simply that they don't understand that when one wants to transcend the ego, it is a tremendous interference to try do this through the intervention of other egos.

Shamcher: Well, I agree with you that when many go to a medium it is not always with a bad intention. But one thing that is going wrong in the first place is that they are thinking of themselves as egos. Inayat Khan never did that, and neither do I. If you call it your ego, and mean something bad, then you have the problem of working against yourself.

I don't think of myself as a despicable being. The Christians do that, unfortunately. They say, I am an awful sinner, there is nothing but sin in me, but Christ is up there and He's all right. Far away, you see, on a pedestal. One needn't do this. It isn't necessary to go the road of thinking of oneself as such a sinner or as an "ego". Rather, without any preconditioning keep your thoughts right. That is the thing, that is real meditation.

And you may sit in a beautiful position to do it if you want, and this is fine if it is comfortable, but you needn't do any particular position. One time when I was with Musharaff and Mahboob Khan, two of Inayat's brothers, I was trying rather desperately to get into the lotus position, and they said, "What are you trying to do, Shamcher?" And I answered, "Well, I'm trying to sit like you." And they laughed and said, "All you have to do is get comfortable. The object is not to sit like us. "

FANA-FI

Jelaluddin: Didn't Inayat Khan set up a program of fana-fi-sheikh, fana-fi-rassoul? That one begins with surrender to a teacher, and then one surrenders to someone of a higher lever, say Inayat Khan or Buddha or someone, a rassoul. Isn't this correct?

Shamcher: That is almost correct. It is a fine way, one of the Sufi ways. Fana-fi-sheikh means you look up to a person as if he were God. You are very noticeable of him, you find him so kind and so generous, that you begin to think that he is so developed that he is a person that you'd rather be than yourself. That is one way.
It is not the only way.

Jelaluddin: Are you saying that it is not necessary?

Shamcher: Yes. Nothing is necessary. This is only one way among many Sufi ways. There is no "way" in fact, that is not a Sufi way.
But let's go on. After fana-fi-sheikh there comes fana-fi-rassoul. Meaning that you can no longer feel that way about one man, or

one teacher, but you can feel that about the theme of the rassoul present in Buddha, Christ, Mohammed or whomever. And then you come to the final surrender in which you are not even satisfied with that. You think, "Well, Buddha was all right, Christ was all right, but I want to surrender to God only, what is called in this progression fana-fi-allah or fana-fi-lillah. This is where you want to end up. There is nothing that says that "this is the way to go and there is no other way." A Sufi doesn't say that. Inayat Khan never said that.

KARMA

Jelaluddin: Since we are speaking of what one has or has not to do, perhaps we should speak about the difference between the idea of Karma ruling our lives, and the Sufi idea of baraka - what I see as a fluid state of grace.

Shamcher: Yes. In the state of enlightenment, Karma disappears. Not only for you but the people around you, for anyone that you may think of. "Karma" is the spiritual equivalent for the old scientific theory of cause and effect. This is Newton's theory. Newton is out now. The new physicist says that there is no such thing as cause and effect. And so it is for the spiritual world. Karma is a concept which is useful to explain certain things about the space in which you live. This doesn't mean that you should believe it. It may be good to say, "I mustn't do that because it will have such and such an effect," but it is also important to understand that there is a definite field to which you are applying the law, and it is not true of the universe as a whole. And also to know that the spiritual path will arrive at a place where you are beyond that.

Jelaluddin: Then some people need it for a time?

Shamcher: Perhaps, but you can't tell a person that he needs it. It is all up to whether they feel that they need it. This then, is his choice.

Jelaluddin: And beyond that feeling?

Shamcher: That is where you can change yourself from a sinner to a saint in one second if you wish, or change the world.

The Mystic Sciences

Jelaluddin: When I heard you speak on the "mystic sciences" the *I Ching,* tarot, astrology, etc. up in Toronto this spring, it kept striking me that you were saying something on a deeper level than that they simply don't have any value. That they could be aids to developing our insight, but the hold of their attraction over us is such that they have degenerated into something much less than they had been intended to be.

Shamcher: Yes. Someone once asked Inayat: "Shouldn't we Sufis get our charts read?" And he answered: "Where are the astrologers?" That is the whole point.
Swami Yukteswar, Yogananda's teacher, once wrote a book called *The Holy Science* that said that Indian astrology, on which is based Western astrology, is about 400,000 years wrong because of a mistake made many, many years ago. The whole idea of zodiacs, twelve zodiacs - why twelve and not a million?

Jelaluddin: I had this explained to me once that the twelve zodiacs correspond to the six chakras below the crown. That there is a masculine and feminine side to each, and the zodiac was an external correspondence to the pathway of our Kundalini energy.

Shamcher: That sounds very good. But some say we have six chakras, some twelve, some three, some four. They are all constructs of the mind, descriptions. Why believe someone else's descriptions? It is better to wait with a judgment until one has gone very deeply into oneself and seen these things. Then, if you see six chakras, of course for you there are six chakras, and if you see three then of course for you there are three. It is different for each person.

Fana-fi (2)

Shamcher: There was one thing that I forgot to say about fani-fi-sheikh and fana-fi-lillah. I was initiated in October of 1923, and then in 1924 saw Inayat Khan again, in Suresnes.

At that time he gave me some practices. One of which was to look at a photograph of him for concentration. And I thought, look at a photograph? What a silly thing! It is impossible to do this, but all right, all right, if he says to do it I'll do it.

And then as I was walking home, there was this great clacking of shoes, on the pavement in back of me, and a man was shouting, "Oh Mr. Beorse, Inayat Khan wants to see you right away." And so I came right back and Inayat said, "Shamcher, I am so sorry, I made a mistake. You should not look at photographs. You should think of the great teachings of the world, those of Buddha, Christ, etc. "

So what he had done was give me the fana-fi-rassoul instead of the fana-fi-sheikh, because he knew it was right for me. What would have happened had he rigidly adhered to the step by step process of fana-fi-sheikh, fana-fi-rassoul, fana-fi-allah?

Jelaluddin: Do you think that he was actually experiencing what you were going through?

Shamcher: Yes. I think he felt the vibrations. He did that always.

Jelaluddin: Again and again in the life of Inayat Khan we see how important his ability to attune himself to vibration was.

Shamcher: Yes. It should be remembered that he was an extremely sensitive musician. Sound and vibration were to him tremendous things. He was more in touch with them than anyone else I've ever seen. He could even use this to throw thoughts into my mind. For example, when I first met him I was to translate his lecture. We didn't get a chance to talk about it. So he just gave the whole lecture, and then I gave the lecture again, in Norwegian. It was really him of course. He had this ability to not only be in touch with me but to completely be in my mind. Nobody else has ever been able to do that..

Jelaluddin: How does this differ from mediumship and the use of oracles?

Shamcher: The Greek oracles used drugs and fumes and things like that. And sometimes they would get into an entirely different world in which they did get in touch with spirits and things on the other side. But what kind do you think? Very crude spirits, and ones that might do the worst things.
Inayat was not like that. He was clear. Sufi means pure, a clear perspective without mixtures of anything. You know, he was the first man I met with whom I felt I could not make circles around him. He knew things. He had the right feeling, and he could make me feel him.

Jelaluddin: When Pir Vilayat gives Darshan, is he attuning himself to vibrations in the same way?

Shamcher: That's what he is trying to do, yes.

Jelaluddin: Or is he predicting?

Shamcher: No, not predicting.

Jelaluddin: In Toronto I heard you say that there is not any such thing as prediction, that the future is fluid and even God doesn't know the future.

Shamcher: Yes, that's my opinion. That's beautiful.

Jelaluddin: That day you disintegrated a certain kind of dependen-

14

cy I had on the *I Ching*. This was very painful at first, but then I felt a tremendous freedom, in the thought that we can make our own future. But you do like the *I Ching* even if you separated me from using it as an oracle, right?

Shamcher: The *I Ching* has beautiful practices which I do. For instance, its practices stressing a breathing out. These practices are in the same vein as spiritual disciplines.

About breath: you know, most people in this culture don't breathe out. In a stingy sense they keep it in, thinking"I have this breath inside, I can't let it out, its very precious." And it is this kind of obsession that some try to overcome when one fasts so long one almost starves, or goes into very prolonged retreat. (One doesn't need to do that, by the way. I have a lot of work, for example, and could never go on a retreat like that, because I have to finish this work while I am still alive.) Anyway, the purpose of these disciplines is to learn how to give up food, to give up air, whatever one is too full of.

Jelaluddin: Would you speak more on darshan?

Shamcher: Yes, in darshan, Inayat would sit with a mureed before him, and he would close his eyes and then the mureed would close his eyes and then suddenly, they would both open their eyes and be in touch - the mureed may not have been in touch but he was in touch - and then Inayat would feel the longing and wishes of the mureed without them being otherwise expressed.

Darshan is not the kind of thing that I would go for, because, in my case at least, it would be a sort of almost an imposition. Rather, I would advise everyone to sit - or stand or whatever - and simply get in touch with what emanates from the silence within them. This is the thing, drop the personality, the worries, everything and just be in touch with that silence within yourself.

And there are many people who understand this.

Jelaluddin: Would you say that this practice breaks up the descriptions we hold of ourselves in our everyday life, and lets us view ourselves once again as a center of possibilities instead of as an object?

Shamcher: I so agree with that! To me now, if you ask who I am, I don't really think that I am anything. But there is a center here that collects, or at least takes charge of a lot of beings - thoughts, feelings and beings. An example of this is how the human body is constantly being served by all of the devoted beings. It is not yourself, really, it is they who take care of you.

People will go to a doctor, and he will say, "Oh, you have a disease!" And they will think, "Oh my goodness, I have a disease! What do I do now?" They shouldn't care about all that. It is these beings that can restore and heal you, and your mind prevents them through fear, and through the thought projected by the doctors saying this and that. In a moment of silence you would feel that you are not really ill.

In the Zikr we say, "This is not my body, this is the temple of God." And you needn't even use the name "god" if that is offensive to you, the important thing to know is that it is a temple, and so it is sacred.

It's really strange when we get caught up in who we think we are, or who others think we are. Take my image for example. If I took these things seriously, I'd have to be a little ashamed. In the first place, because all the descriptions are wrong since I don't really exist, in the second place because I can never live up to what I am supposed to do. Too much is expected of one, one can't do all that, and so one is always a disappointment to somebody else . When this happens, it is time to think, well if I am all that important than at least I'm somebody, and then it doesn't matter anymore.

Jelaluddin: The key - the attachment to the description?

Shamcher: Yes.

Jelaluddin: Could you give us an example of someone being too attached to fruits?

16

Shamcher: Yes. I have a friend who is an economist. I consider him the finest economist in the United States. He is also a zen man, and interested in Sufism and Yoga.

One day he comes to me and says, "Bryn, I don't think I will continue any longer." I don't give him any response. "Yes," he says, "I have articles running in the Economic journal, and I have written three books, but nobody listens. Nobody does what I ask. I think I'll give up." "Why do you want to give up?" I say, "Look how hard I have worked all my life. And yet the only thing that I can do is to continue with what believe in for the rest of my life, and the less people who listen the more intensely must I work."

So he says, "But Bryn, you are one in a million, no I mean one in a billion." But anyway he realized that he had made a mistake by saying that he was going to give up.

Jelaluddin: We have spoken a great deal about attachments. Would you say that even if people cannot dissolve their attachments, they would become much better off if they could simply make them more gentle?

Shamcher: I think so, yes, definitely. Too often the trouble is that we want a sudden change into something impossible, we want a pedestal, so that is true. We can develop right here and now, if not perfectly, at least gradually.

Jelaluddin: We spoke of disease. Would you say that a person can cure himself?

Shamcher: In the first place, whatever name you put on a disease is laughable. People say, "Oh, cancer. That can't be cured. " Who knows what cancer means? And who knows that can't be cured? Everything can be and has been completely cured at different times. And any disease that you can name has been completely cured by some people. The reason that there is so little of it now is that there is so little faith in these things.

There is a sort of faith in medical science, and of course some of the doctors in this field are the finest people in the world. And of them the very finest admit that they cannot answer questions like this, because they only know one dimension of healing and that is not entirely natural.

I know of one of these men, a Dr. Simonton, who has taken on any cancer patient who is given up by regular doctors, and then he makes them develop their thought power - their heart and thought power combined - and then really look at themselves. A phenomenally high percentage have been cured. He has even described cases in which a cancerous growth has diminished in a week or a month into nothing.

Or there is the story of the yogi in India who had his hand cut off by the police who thought he was a criminal. And then the policeman said, "Oh, I'm sorry, you're not the right person!" But the yogi told him not to worry about it, held the arm back in place for awhile, sitting there, and in half an hour there wasn't a sign.

This is the ability the human body has in it. And we have not been utilizing it - though it is perhaps not so bad. Humanity has gone into an anti-spiritual development for awhile to find the "facts" of life, and now, gradually, we are returning to that more keen understanding of what life is all about, and the amazing things that our bodies can do.

DEATH

Jelaluddin: How about death?

Shamcher: That is another reason for the misunderstanding. Death is a different thing than we usually picture it. And death doesn't come from a disease. A disease may come at the same time, and then people will say, "Oh, he died from cancer." You can't prevent death, and why should you want to? That is why healing groups make a great mistake when they say, "These people mustn't die, we must heal them." Cancer may be a hideous disease, but there is nothing hideous about death. It is merely a certain rhythm which says, "Now this form of life is out."

Many people ask about Inayat Khan's death. Well, there are many theories, but I see that he had simply lived out his life. He wasn't physically exhausted or anything like that, in fact he was fresh enough to be able to go to India and live a comfortable last year there, but his life as a constant stimulator of people's vibrations was finished. So he said as he went to India that he wanted no one to go with him. A couple of disciples disobeyed.

Jelaluddin: Had you intimations of his death before it came?

Shamcher: Well, one time he said to me, "Murshid has no more interest," and I had a feeling about it then, and another time when I told him that I was looking forward to meeting him the following summer he said, "From now on, Shamcher, we will meet in your intuition."

Jelaluddin: Did you say once that he died of a broken heart?

Shamcher: No, I never said that, that was ----- who said that.

Jelaluddin: Some say that he was poisoned.

Shamcher: These are all superstitions. He was very happy that last year, and when he died there was the scent of roses in the room.

Jelaluddin: What are your thoughts on your own death?

Shamcher: Oh, I was in it once, when I had my accident, and the doctors told my children that I was dead. And during that time I met my parents and everything was fine, but then I was insolent enough to come back.
That experience of death was a very pleasant thing. My mother and father spoke to me as if I had been there with them all the time. They weren't surprised, and the whole thing felt like it was just a continuation of a conversation. Probably I had been there before and not remembered it. Or perhaps without being aware of it.

19

By the way, when you were speaking about the mystic sciences before, were you including the atomic theory and the Quantum theory? I would include these as well. Because when you have a light photon you can explain it mathematically as a wave, that is, you have a certain set of equations which describe it as a wave, but then simultaneously you have another set of equations that describe it as a particle, an entirely different set of equations. So the old physicists say, the ones still bound to the old form of cause and effect, that this is impossible, it can't be two things. But the Quantum theory people say, "Yes, the two things seemingly opposite are two poles of the same reality. "

In a sense we can explain it like this. Imagine you have a circle. When you look at it from the end it looks like a straight line. So in this dimension it is just a line. But stand it up in the second dimension and it appears as the circle. Now, if you put it in the third dimension you may have a doughnut; cut a line through it, you have two circles, but actually these two circles are just another way of expressing the doughnut in the third dimension.

Jelaluddin: I am always very interested when we talk about the concept of opposites. Isn't that how linguistics tries to explain language, as a system embodying a relationships of opposites?

Shamcher: Yes, language is built on the relationship of opposites, but not so much in Chinese or the other Oriental languages as our own.

Jelaluddin: I found that out a couple of years ago when I worked for a time as a Vietnamese interpreter. Those languages are so much more fluid and less suggestive of what we sometimes call the "subject-object dichotomy".

A line from Hazrat Inayat Khan has just entered my head here. He says, "Everything is apprehended by its opposite, And that's why God is so hard to apprehend because He has no opposites."

Shamcher: That's very good. That's very true. It is we who are living in the opposites. Good or evil, dark or light.

Jelaluddin: What is enlightenment?

Shamcher: Oh, enlightenment, yes. Well, let us just say that enlightenment is something you are looking forward to, and when you reach it then you can begin looking forward to the next enlightenment. You see, there is always more.
Even God himself gets better all the time! When you have begun to be enlightened you feel, "Yes, I have a lot more to learn, but now at least I am happy because there is no doubt anymore." And in this state you can look at the mistakes you have made, and passed and know that they are fine, that they belong. So you are enlightened in the sense that your doubts aren't giving you such trouble, and you are ready to begin learning a thousand things.

Jelaluddin: Enlightenment is the point at which you realize that you don't know?!

Shamcher: Ya! (chuckles)

Jelaluddin: There is something that happens like that in initiation, where you begin to "know that you don't know" only it's so sudden that it can be tremendously confusing. After I was initiated by Neaatma at that Canada camp, the same time that I met you, Shamcher, I entered a period of bewilderment in which I felt completely disconnected from my normal habits and routines. Like I am a writer, and I couldn't get myself to sit down and write, except for brief intense bursts, for about four months!
Now I think that a lot of what was happening to me was that I was learning to communicate without words, what the Sufis call "tawwajeh" or heart to heart, and in the midst of this lesson I couldn't immerse myself in the same old ways of analyzing and describing everything. It's not painful to me anymore. Probably because I am finally coming out of it. But what would you say to someone who is still going through it?

Shamcher: You just have to wait, be in touch with the silences as we've talked about, and it will work itself out.

Jelaluddin: Is that all? Do you think it is bad to struggle against it?

Shamcher: Yes. That is useless, and will make the experience worse.

Jelaluddin: I wish I understood this more. The point where I stopped being angry with myself for being unable to transmit the images that I was being bombarded with through my pen, to just feeling wonderful about the deep change that was going on in my being.

Shamcher: You know, this is really wonderful for me to hear. I didn't realize that the initiations being given by the present initiators could still do that. When I was initiated by Inayat, I hung around in Suresnes for six weeks and then - blam!

REINCARNATION

Jelaluddin: What do you think of reincarnation, Shamcher?

Shamcher: The Soul may be thought of as something individual regarding you, but the Soul is also something deeper, and in this sense the soul is the same Soul for everyone. And in this sense the soul doesn't reincarnate, it receives an impression. It gathers around it impressions, or vibrations you may call them, of heart and mind and body.
Take as an example a soul that is coming to the world of matter to make and receive impressions again. On the way it meets the soul of Beethoven, which is departing. Beethoven doesn't need his music anymore, which is a product of the vibrations of his mind and heart, and so he sheds the impression that is his music, like a coat he no longer needs. And the soul that is approaching the physical

world, and wants things of this sort, looks at this field of vibrations and thinks, "This is good, I like this," and so he absorbs a little of the coat and comes here and plays like Beethoven, and then people say, "It is Beethoven reincarnated!" Even this soul may begin to think it is Beethoven reincarnated, but it is not, it is an impression of Beethoven in the form of vibrations of his mind and heart.

There is reincarnation, but not in the sense that some of us super-ficially believe. There isn't a changing soul that comes down and then goes up again, the soul is more aloof and impersonal than that. It is sort of sitting there and looking down on the whole play.

Just look at the way the idea of reincarnation is sometimes abused in India: They see a man crawling along in the street, with leprosy, stretching out a half-broken arm, but the Indians say, "That's his own fault, he did something wrong in his last life and so he re-incarnates in this form." That's superstition and cruelty and not reincarnation!

Jelaluddin: How does the Soul get here in the first place?

Shamcher: The Soul exists forever and has no beginning or end, or at least any beginning or end that anyone here can imagine.

Jelaluddin: Then why does it take a body?

Shamcher: To get experience. A metaphor would be that you have a finger, and then you put a glove on it, and stick it down in some hot water to experience the feeling. The Soul makes this kind of impression in this world of mind and matter to sift up the experi-ence. That is why God has created the universe in the first place. And why he is continually creating it through each soul.

Jelaluddin: I don't really understand what you are trying to say about reincarnation and the Soul.

Shamcher: What I think doesn't matter. But what I am trying to do here is to quote Inayat Khan: that the Soul is part of the eternal God, the Light. It is in a sense One with God, and in a sense it is separate. And, as we said before, every opposite thing is really part of the same thing. The Soul doesn't have any opposite. It doesn't go down or up. The Soul is immovable. It doesn't need to move.

Jelaluddin: Is the Soul in the body?

Shamcher: Only insofar as it gives the body life. For instance the moment that you die there is nothing in it. You may picture it as you want. No one can draw an adequate picture from the physical world that can truly explain it. You can picture it all you want, but there is no final understanding of it. For instance, is it like that wall over there? These kind of things can't be answered. Perhaps one could say that as the flower has a fragrance, so the body has a "fragrance" which is the Soul. The Soul is a very subtle vibration which is too subtle for our minds to comprehend.

Jelaluddin: How about the concepts of Soul and spirit. Is there any difference?

Shamcher: Not really. Sometimes they are not used synonymously, but there is no real difference, or the difference is too subtle for us to appreciate.

Jelaluddin: From what you've said, it would seem that you don't accept the idea that reincarnation is a process by which we are attempting to reach perfection.

Shamcher: The soul may try various impressions to attain to more knowledge, but not really perfection. Is there anything you can call perfection? One of the silliest notions going around in this line is, "Well, he is a perfect master." There is no such thing as a master, except maybe in shoemaking, mechanics or making books perhaps. When you come to a spiritual life there is never a master, there never was and never will be a master. As Inayat Khan said: "There is only One master, the spirit that leads every Soul towards its destination." "Master" is a spiritual concept and nothing more, and to hear people talk about the "perfect master", so very sad.

OBSESSION

Jelaluddin: The condition that Inayat Khan refers to as obsession: *The course of some people who are apt to understand The Message of God as the message of the mediums. They understand the Message the same way they understand an obsession; a man who is obsessed with a philosopher begins to speak philosophy, and when his obsession is gone he can no longer talk about it. It is true, that persons who are in this condition will speak most intelligently on philosophy and metaphysics in the time that they are obsessed. But then, when the obsession is gone, they are just like a horse without a rider; when they speak they are not themselves. This kind of thing has nothing to do with the prophetic message. God does not take hold of a certain body in order to give his message to the world. This is to be distinctly understood.*

Shamcher: Inayat Khan spent the last four hours of his time talking to us about mediums, and explaining that many mediums have contact with spirits, but which spirits? There is so much cheating and confusion on the other side. Genuine teachers speak to their pupils directly if they want to make contact after they have left their body. Nevertheless, we have the incident that happened after Inayat's death, where four of his closest disciples came forth with messages from him they "received' through mediums.

I know of a Turkish psychiatrist who travelled the world looking for people with psychic gifts. You know what she found? That the professional soothsayers, mediums and predicters had practically no ability but there were all kinds of gifted people among doctors, nurses, teachers and ordinary working people. But these people knew enough to keep their powers hidden.

As far as the prophetic message is involved, this is an admonition to help us remember that contact with the other side means nothing. It may even be dangerous, since there are all kinds of communication that are destructive.

ANOTHER KIND OF OBSESSION

Jelaluddin: That has triggered two thoughts: would you say that mediums are sort of dead to the possibility of making the future; and can we connect this idea of obsession, i. e. the entrance of something from the other side, with the kind of obsession that is the rigid adherence to a conceptual framework?

Shamcher: Most mediums, and so many mystics who "predict the future" instead of helping to be creators of it, are dead to it. And it is a pity that we listen so much to them and that they get so much space in the papers as opposed to those who are really trying to do something.

Let us take the area of engineering and physics with which I am acquainted. When a man has created something, that thing, and his opinion of it, weighs more than a thousand bureaucrats who pronounce judgment as to whether it is good or bad. How can they know anything about it? And yet it is the bureaucrats and the president, or whomever, who gets listened to, as if they know more than the man who has spent years and years doing the research, even sometimes when the researcher is backed by his university, or many universities across the country. It is the scientists who can judge on the basis of the sciences, and their opinion should weigh more than 1,000 bureaucrats, but such is not the case. I know of one case where seven major universities and four research departments of industrial companies recommended that a certain thing be done, and yet nothing happened because we had to wait for someone from the office of technical assessment, or some congressmen, or the president's energy czar to come and tell us whether it was really any good!

This is the same kind of obsession, on another plane, that Inayat Khan was speaking about. Some are obsessed with voices from the other side, some are obsessed with the bureaucracy or the government. Both are dependent on an external authority that has been chosen on the flimsiest excuse. Consider the way it works with research, for example. The University sends in a request saying, "We need such and such an amount of money to complete our research." It goes to Bert Lance or some other budget director, and he, on the basis of completely inadequate experience decides what should and should not be researched. And he complains that if everyone got his way with research, we would have ten times as big a budget for research projects. Well, that's excellent, that's just what we need! It is research and investigation that will bring us out of our inflation because then we would be actively doing [words missing here].

The true economists can explain this. But we listen to the economic opinion of a congressman who has arranged for his salary to increase in correspondence with the inflation, though it is exactly these increases that are causing the inflation. "Oh, he can't live on $43,000; he must have $58,000!" But we who live on less than $10,000 wonder about these wonderful economic experts who are so stupid they couldn't get by when they were making only $43,000.

And this is just an illustration of a principle expressed in our society. There are many cases that are the same, because there is nothing in the society that is not sacred, which is not as relevant to our spiritual development as the things spoken about by "spiritual people".

Jelaluddin: Shamcher, I feel we're approaching something here that is an important part of where I want this book to go. To understand that obsession is something much more than simply giving too much authority to beings from the other side. That we are also "obsessed" when we give that power away to people on this side.

Shamcher: Yes. Like in the example of the congressmen and the energy people etc. When we give absolute authority to any "expert" we are obsessed in a sense.

Jelaluddin: I don't think this covers what I mean, but we can return to it. Will you talk about how we are to understand the difference between an intuition that is growing more powerful as we walk on the spiritual path, and the presence of beings from the other side in our consciousness? I don't personally find this very easy. Sometimes, because I am using another part of the mind than the one usually associated with the ego part when I am using my intuition, it almost seems that I am hearing voices, or receiving instructions.

Shamcher: You must very carefully judge here yourself. Don't be afraid to do this. Many people don't judge, even many Sufis, and they will say to themselves, "Oh, I had a vision while I was meditating, so that must be right." It isn't always right.

A vision may be a spirit that is very eager to come in, or it may be simply a thought of your own that is interfering with your intuition. There is no way to tell this except by exercising your own powers of judgment. If you go running off to other people to tell you about your own spirit then you are weakening your powers every time you listen to such a person. Remember Buddha's farewell address. This gets a little bit difficult when you think about your teacher. But remember, the teacher is not someone who should tell you what to do. If he does tell you what to do then he is not a teacher. A teacher is one who helps you evolve and awaken your own latent powers of judgment and decision.

Jelaluddin: Well, Shamcher, I must say that things are not always like that within the Sufi Orders that I know. And oftentimes I see a greater interest in finding someone to act as an authority then actual self investigation.

Shamcher: Yes, well this natural, and it is only the people who expect Sufis to suddenly be angels who are disappointed. One should not be concerned with all the apparent conflict within the Sufi order, but rather be encouraged by how much real service there is. For example, this conflict between SIRS and the Sufi Order is of minor importance in my view. I am more concerned with all these people we've been talking about who are running to soothsayers and people outside for help.

Jelaluddin: Do you feel that one should not seek help then, from the beings of the other side?

Shamcher: Yes, it's not to be sought. It will come of itself at the right time and then you will act on it. For example, Pir Vilayat came to me once and said, "I meditated on my father and he indicated to me that I was doing a wrong by not believing in the ranks and titles; if I follow that line I will destroy the order and there will just be little flowers here and there instead of a concentrated Order." And he may be right or wrong but he'd had the feeling that this had come from his father, something very understandable, that a man who was trying to spread the message of his father would want to be led by his father.

Jelaluddin: Do you think that he was really in communication with his father?

Shamcher: Yes! Everybody is, everybody who has ever been initiated is in communication with Inayat Khan. In fact, Inayat once said: "People who have never seen me, who will be born after I've left, may often be in closer contact with me than you people who have known my person, because you will confuse me with my physical person."

INTUITION

Jelaluddin: When one uses his intuition, sometimes it is hard to distinguish between spiritual guidance and the guidance that has been set up by the vibratory field of Inayat Khan and his teachings.

Shamcher: There is no distinction. There is definitely a set of vibrations that have been set in motion by Inayat Khan and his pupils. And anyone can tune into these.
But there is one thing that I will say about questions of this type.
All these things are subtle, and you can't get a sudden easy answer, you have to discover the answer gradually for yourself. And then

you may discover it to complete satisfaction, many have done that. But it is a gradual process, and so you shouldn't feel discouraged if you are not entirely clear about it now.

It is not clear in any language, but it can become clear to you.

Jelaluddin: Isn't it possible that you will need a human guide before you begin to tune in to these subtler vibrations?

Shamcher: I don't think so. Others may feel this, but I definitely believe not. Rabindranath Tagore said in one of his poems that they had told him that he had to go through this gate or that gate or follow this leader to become close to God, but then God had grace on him and led him to Himself without any guide.

Jelaluddin: Well, it seems to me that you're acting as a guide when you tell us not to follow guides!

Shamcher: No, what I say here is not for the purpose of guiding you. I express what I feel because I have been asked to, and one may or may not listen to that as they wish. That is not the same as guidance. The purpose is very important.

Jelaluddin: Back to obsessions: do you sometimes pick up on others' pain and sorrows?

Shamcher: Yes, that is very possible. Inayat Khan did that all the time. And when that happens you have the right to notice it and not engage in it thereby ridding yourself of it, or you decide that that is a delightful feeling and go about discovering it more deeply.

Jelaluddin: Do people sometimes make you take on these feelings?

Shamcher: No. Some people have superstitions about these types of influences. They say, "This man is a vampire, he takes all my powers!" Well, I say to these people that if anyone is taking your powers its your own damn fault! No one can take your powers if you don't let them, and besides, it is not that he has taken your power, it is that you have emptied yourself of it to him for some reason.

Jelaluddin: I feel this is a crucial point. Obsession is always volitional, and if the obsession is of the type where spirits enter, it is because we have invited them in, wouldn't you say?

Shamcher: Right.

Jelaluddin: Is there a difference between obsession and possession?

Shamcher: Obsession applies to things of the earth as well as things of the inner plane. For example, it may mean obsession with an idea, or obsession with the authority of the worldly hierarchies, such as when we spoke of bureaucrats and the congress etc., as well as the other kind of obsession which means to be obsessed by a spirit. But possession as far as I understand it refers only to that instance where a spirit has possessed you.

Jelaluddin: This is what I was trying to get at once before, Shamcher. The more subtle side of obsession that deals with ideas and things rather than dealings with the other side. An example of what I'm thinking of could be the way an artist can become obsessed with his art, a poet can become obsessed with the need to make poetry, or a person can become obsessed with sex or romantic love. We can go on and on. Obsession with drugs, obsession with one particular teacher. The common factor seems to be that they are rigidities that thwart enlightenment. And yet they are, I believe, a necessary part of the process by which we learn, so they are a sort of positive obsession which are our, perhaps, best opportunities if we can only look at them in the right way. (answered somewhere else)

Darshan

Jelaluddin: People could perhaps misunderstand darshan as an obsession.

Shamcher: Darshan is communication between two beings, and shouldn't be thought of as anything else. I have described to you how Inayat Khan used the darshan, how you and he would suddenly open your eyes and look into each other. Some people got no feeling from such darshans and others felt their lives had been changed, that they had experienced a part of his mind and gotten from it just what they wanted, and were very happy because of it.

Jelaluddin: Perhaps the difference we could say was that such darshan is real with living beings, and there was no intrusion from the outside, that Inayat Khan was in a sense merely carrying out his role as a teacher and reflecting back to his pupils deeper sides of themselves that they were perhaps even aware of.

Mediums

Jelaluddin: Have you heard of David Spangler?

Shamcher: I read a recent article by him in *The Message,* and I thought that was pretty good.

Jelaluddin: Do you know that he claims to have direct contact with beings, or a being, that is trying to bring about the "new age" on this planet?

Shamcher: So many people these days claim to have direct contact. As soon as you try to express the contact, everything becomes tilted with one's own stupid personality. So, for instance, 50,000 initiates claim to have contact with Inayat Khan. This is true, but because everyone is different everyone interprets what they feel a little differently. They are entitled to this, but not to go around and say 'I have the contact', as if it were the only one. Which is not to say anything against David Spangler. If he said this it was probably as a sort of approximate statement. Nobody correctly represents another being, whether in another world or even here. Like when someone comes and says he is representing President Carter, he is lying if he says that he is speaking on the president's behalf. He may not know he is lying when he does this, but it is so nevertheless. How can he represent him when he can't react the same way that Carter would? It is the same way with spiritual beings.

Another example of this was Edgar Cayce. who also thought he had direct contact. He had to go into trance, and then he transferred something. Yes, he transferred beautiful messages from the other side and maybe the fact that he was in a trance kept out some of the tilting towards personality that usually goes on, so parts of them were accurate. However, he made all kinds of predictions also about things of which he had no idea, and which were completely false. This is the trouble with people who "channel." They forget that their inspiration is always colored by their own particular experience and tilted to their own ideas.

Jelaluddin: Do you think that some mediums are better than others though?

Shamcher: Yes, and I've spoken about Eileen Garrett. The most famous are not the best.

Jelaluddin: How about Jane Roberts who wrote *Seth Speaks*?

Shamcher: Oh no, that's very tilted.

Jelaluddin: But what was it she was hearing? Didn't things come through her?

Shamcher: Of course they came through her, and through her picked up all kinds of mistakes and idiosyncrasies.

Jelaluddin: It seems to me that what you are saying is that the only way to keep your balance and also be in touch with the other side is to do it in silent meditation, for as soon as you try and articulate it, it is interfered with.

Shamcher: True.

Jelaluddin: Is this because in that particularly beautiful kind of silence there is no voice there attaching importance. Like your ego is there saying, "Well, what benefit can I get out of this?"

Shamcher: Yes, yes.

Jelaluddin: What do you mean by co-creation?

Shamcher: Simply, when a friend of mine works on a solar device and I work on OTEC. On a deeper level, when the same ideas are being worked on by Trimble, Heronomus and myself simultaneously. God doesn't make anything directly, he does it through people: that's co-creation.

Jelaluddin: The future is fluid.

Shamcher: Yes, that's right.

Power (exoteric)

Jelaluddin: Do we have power over the elements?

Shamcher: We don't have power over them. If we behave right they will gladly cooperate with us. The elements have much more power than the present civilization. We have very little power even over ourselves. Even over our health and bodies. We are almost morons in the way we behave, and the elements are much more effective in their operations than we in ours. Although we could become even better than the elements in time.

Jelaluddin: Can humans concentrate on bringing rain?

Shamcher: Of course. Don't you know that the Indians have done that for ages with their dances? Their dances express what they deeply feel. But it is not really the dances but their minds which are enticed by the dances which are making the rain.

Jelaluddin: This is what I've always heard you say about exoteric forms. It is not the dance but what the dance invokes. Would you speak on obsession and exoteric forms?

Shamcher: Yes. The exoteric form is the outer ritual that you see. For example, people taking part in parades, and the rituals one uses at devotional services. These are what one would call obsessional when the persons doing it are not aware of the symbolism and essence within it. They think that the services and the parades themselves are the essential meaning, and this may be dangerous.

The more so when the exoteric form involves the structure of society, and how that structure interacts with peoples' lives.

I already gave you the example where the government believes itself capable of deciding which scientific technologies are important enough to be developed, whether they know anything about the particular technology or not. By adhering to the form of the society, or what people have come to believe is the form, people resign themselves to the decision of the government without questioning the process by which the decision has been reached, and hence we are stuck on the rather low level of technological advancement that we have today. This goes for church organizations too, the way people will believe that a man simply because he has the title of Bishop or something must be right.

In Sufi organizations of course, we are supposed to be better off than this because we are particularly aware of the unity of things.

But there is even there some of this happening, and there are people who take it very seriously when someone who seems to have a higher responsibility says something. But actually the "higher responsibility" in the given situation means nothing more than someone had the particular idea that something should be said. Everyone has the right to say what he feels; in fact it is his duty to see that it gets said. You have the right not to believe that a certain thing must be right or wrong simply because a certain person has said it. Everything which is expressed in words is of rather inferior quality anyway. And it should be remembered that nothing that has ever happened is important, it has been made to be important.

Jelaluddin: It would seem that the exoteric form and the authority of the hierarchy are actually the lesser part of the Message. Like they are the discriminatory part of the mind which divides things into compartments so they may be communicable in words. But it is really the heart, the essence and the feeling which is the most important. How does this fit in all the recent talk of "resigning initiation" from the Sufi Order, Shamcher?

Shamcher: No one has a right to tell a person what he should or should not do, but the person himself. And as for initiation, initiation is as much as the initiated one accepts of the initiation, and nothing else and nothing more. Some are now afraid that initiation obliges a man to acknowledge his membership in a certain order. An initiator may think so, but in that fact I feel sorry for him. The only thing that initiation makes is a contact, which may be very important, or it may be rather unimportant, it all depends. For instance, initiation into the Sufi Order may mean that your spiritual contact has been cleaned up. That now you are better able to keep out the undesirable spirits and be close to the sincere, knowledgeable and desirable ones. Anyone can get in touch with Inayat Khan or his teacher, Seyyed Madani, or any of the spiritual beings, for example, but if you are initiated it is easier because you have been reminded to them. Your name has been told. And so from that point it is easier to be in contact with them. It may be easier the more sincere you were in the moment of initiation. But once you have had that initiation no one can take it away from you. It goes beyond lifetimes.

Jelaluddin: So in a sense initiation is being completed in other realms, something much more than where anyone could simply say whether one is officially a Sufi or not.

Shamcher: Yes, it should be that. It isn't always. It depends on both the initiate and the initiator. It is meant to attune your vibrations to the Order, and it sometimes does.

Jelaluddin: Would you say that from the original moment of Bayat every successive step on the Sufi path is really a movement towards freedom, a movement towards what you've called elsewhere the fluid future, dispensing of the rigidities and obsessions that have prevented one from their natural contact with God?

Shamcher: That's really true. Excellent! One who was initiated by Inayat Khan would say that.

Karma

Jelaluddin: Fritjof Capra, in the *Tao of Physics*, says in one place that we are trapped in our own conceptual framework, and that when we transcend words and explanations we obtain liberation and break the bonds of karma.

Shamcher: The idea of karma is connected with the so-called dogma of cause and effect. In the West this has been developed in science through Isaac Newton, and for a long time scientists believed that everything contained the laws of cause and effect, but recently a small group of physicists have begun to realize that this is not so.
When you explain things you are bound to use language. And in language you are using something that is based partly on cause and effect and many other dogmas. When you realize this truth you

become like some people of the East, and of the West too, who say, "It can't be explained." The best you can do is sort of run around it and speak of it in metaphors, and hope that people will get to it through that. Language uses the law of cause and effect, which is the same thing as karma. When you transcend it, other laws become applicable.

Physics hasn't been able to tell us which laws these are yet, but it has discovered that all these concepts and dogmas and so called natural laws were never really laws at all, they were only our own ideas.

Jelaluddin: And to break out of this trap is to go inward, the silence?

Shamcher: Silence yes, but especially a realization that your ideas of cause and effect and karma are nothing more than conceptual structures of your mind which have been used for the purpose of instruction but are not "final truths". They have been used by your mind as instruments of attainment. And in using your mind it appears that it has become bound to your civilization's concepts of how to understand life, but when you begin to see from the point of view of Tao that it really hasn't been. Which doesn't mean that you are suddenly enlightened and can see everything. But it is the first step. To see that everything you've thought is not necessarily so.

It is interesting today that some physicists are seeing that, just as the ancient sages did. And in a sense just as clearly, but in another sense not as clearly. They are complaining, for example, that they don't have the capacity to visualize in the fourth dimension as they believe the ancients did. And perhaps some of them did, but there certainly must have been great discrepancies also in the manner in which they realized this. We needn't think that these people suddenly came into a complete understanding of everything. Some saints' understanding was better than others, but there is no area in which everything is understood by someone.

Jelaluddin: Does this fit in with the idea that some people have that there has to be a form to believe in God?

Shamcher: Yes, or rather they like to have a form. But some people are very simple and don't need that ever. This not a matter of intellectual achievement. Some highly intellectual people still live with forms, and not only don't understand but actually have a contempt for the present no-form concepts.

Jelaluddin: Another thing which Capra says, "The void gives birth to an infinite variety of form, which it sustains and then eventually reabsorbs."

Shamcher: This is another way of expressing the ancient concept of Brahma coming into existence in the world and then withdrawing again so nothing exists. And then he comes into the world again and then withdraws again. A great rhythm, and each period, called in the ancient mythology a Kalpa.

Jelaluddin: Is this contrary to the theory of relativity, or the "big-bang" theory of creation held by some scientists?

Shamcher: No, There are at least two possibilities connected with the theory of relativity. One is that the world is continually and forever expanding; the other is that it expands and then contracts, and then expands again. And this is the same as the ancient sages believe in, and let us say that it is the same as I believe in.

Jelaluddin: It sounds like breathing!

Shamcher: Yes, breathing is exactly the same thing. You expand when you breathe out and things scatter, and then you breathe in and you contract. This is true on the other planes of existence, that is correct. And then with your last breath, it is only the last breath of the physical body, you continue to breathe with your subtler bodies.

Jelaluddin: How can I know this is true if I haven't experienced it?

Shamcher: There is no need to. You shouldn't believe in something before you have discovered it. For the time being, the healthiest thing to say is, "I reserve judgment". Some people have become convinced from books, sometimes so much so that they don't want it anymore and begin to fight it, like the man who said to Jesus,"I believe, I believe, please help my un-belief!" That is one of the preliminary stages, and it is healthier in a sense and more balanced. When you come to look at something you should say, "I don't know this but I will find out, or I may find out."

Jelaluddin: Let's talk about balance, Shamcher.

Shamcher: Yes. Hazrat Inayat Khan often said that "the message for today is balance". And he meant that in many ways. For example the balance between heart and mind. This kind of balance emanates from yourself and not from adventuresome spirits on the other side.

He also meant by this: balancing your being in the world with your work on yourself. Some people think that they can't do anything for the world until they have perfected their work on themselves. Well, there is no way of perfecting yourself except through working in the world. That's why we are here. If you don't want to work in the world before you have perfected yourself, you might just as well have remained outside it. You didn't have to be born. To me, this has become more and more clear the longer I live. You work on yourself by achieving the little things in your home, among your coworkers etc. And yet so many teachers today are telling pupils to take long vacations or retreats and so on. In Inayat's time we had a summer school which was like a vacation, but apart from that we had no retreats.

But I must admit at this point that when I was younger, around 18 or 19 (this was before I met Inayat Khan), I was a student at the university and very, very busy and suddenly I thought, "I can't stand it anymore, I must go." And so I put on my skis (I didn't want any transportation - no buses or trains for me!), and walked into the mountains towards a white beautiful one I saw far, far away. These were the Trolheimin mountains, which means "home of the trolls".

Anyway it took me weeks, and some would say later, "You went into the mountains in the wintertime? You must be crazy!" And in a sense I might have been crazy.

A dog came along who had the same kind of urge that I was having, and I saw this and tried to push him back but he kept with me anyway. And then we had a terrific snowstorm, and we had to go against it for days and days, usually not knowing whether we were going up hill or downhill, the storm was so strong. Finally one day I thought to myself, "I can't last anymore. Let me just go over to those rocks and lie down."

It is known to the people of those parts that it is very dangerous to go to sleep in a snowstorm in the mountains but I had no thought of this, none at all. Anyway, I went to the rocks, but they turned out not to be rocks. I fell down and stood before a little door, and there was a cabin there. I knocked on the cabin door and heard bare feet running over the stone floor, and then the door was opened, and I was invited inside and slept in the hayloft. In the morning we had a beautiful breakfast of goat's milk and things, and so I said, "Now what should I pay you?" And they laughed and said they couldn't use my money up there anyway, and they never went down into town, not for the last ten years when they first came up from the valley. But they said that I could pay them 25 cents if I wanted to feel that I had paid them something.

And so after tramping around in the mountains I returned to civilization, the first sign of it being the smell of coffee. Though all the impressions of civilization are thrust at you again, you are a different person. For two or three weeks, I was what the sages call enlightened, that is, nothing affected me. Before this, when I looked at women, I would say, "How can I stand not coming very much closer to her?" But now there was no such question inside me. I enjoyed her beauty, she meant nothing more to me, everything in life was in calm balance. I needed this for my balance at that time, and maybe many people do need it, and I think they should obey the urge when it comes.

It is by knowing when I should go to the mountains or the beach, that all my life I have stayed not in good balance but fair balance all the time. But the balance that is required to root up your earthly desires, comes from looking at your person as something that you are not too much concerned about. Later in life this came to me, and I realized that this person is not really "Mr. so and so".

And through this I have gradually come to discover the numerous agents of the body that keep it in shape, and became friendly with them instead of opposing them. It is through this that you become a master of yourself and have balance. Everything is an attitude of the mind, and this "mind" that I am talking about of course is the mind and heart.

Jelaluddin: Shamcher, if disease is, as you say, an attitude of mind, why then are not all people who have faith and want to be healed, healed?

Shamcher: I have never met a person, including myself, who has faith in the complete sense. It is something one can develop but faith doesn't mean to say "I believe in God." That is not faith, that is not balance. The balance is to flow with the universal process.

Jelaluddin: Obsession in a sense is when one can't tear himself away from the sense of physical pain of the body, or at least this is a good metaphor for it.

Shamcher: Yes, it is very difficult when you have physical pain. The war was a great test of that. Some were tortured, and it is worse in a sense when a person is imposing the pain, but some people even used this to help them develop. There was a person in Norway who was repeatedly tortured by the Nazis and knew he would be tortured again. And when I asked him how he could stand it he said, "There comes a point when all these things don't matter to you."

"But the pain," I said. And he answered me that half of the pain was the fear of death.

"I don't fear death anymore so there is only half the pain. It is bearable. And I now know only one thing, I will never give out a name or anything else they want of me."

What do you think of this man? I don't know if he was a Sufi, but that is the kind of balance that is required.

Jelaluddin: A tremendous sense of balance! He had been at the extremes, and learned not to fear them. Perhaps we can say that such extreme things are very useful, in that when one returns from them your balance is so deep, because you have felt what it is like to be at the poles.

Shamcher: That is very true. There is of course not a single thing in this life which does not have a purpose and which does not help the soul in its development. Even the wildest kinds of obsessions, even those states of the mind that may cause you to be put in a hospital, are useful. Many psychiatrists say these days that they are not only useful, they are in a sense superior to ordinary experience, in what they help you become afterwards. They are looking at them insofar as they bring you to mystical balance.

Obsession, like everything else in life, helps the community and the individual advance and to realize the need for balance. For example schizophrenics and depressed maniacs, they are supposed to be so bad, but they are often actually helping themselves and those around them to reach the state of mystical balance by taking another path.

One time a friend of mine was in a hospital, and I heard a group of psychiatrists talking. They were talking about a physicist who had come in and told them, "You know, this table isn't really a fixed table. I put my hand on it and I feel the sub-atomic particles running down from my hand meeting the particles running up from the table. And some interpret this as a calm solid surface but it really isn't." And these psychiatrists were laughing at this poor physicist for being off his mind! He was actually explaining the truth, but

43

they didn't realize it. He had schizophrenia they said.

It is the same in the case of many others. Fortunately it is realized now by many psychiatrists that schizophrenics have reached another end of the balance and together with what is called his "sane" state, which is not so sane, he is working towards a new balance.

Excuse me, I was thinking of another question you asked me, the one about faith. Well, do we mean 'faith' in the sense that a person will visit a dear saints' burial place and get in touch with him through the body that is left there? A lot of saints and sages in the past have left their bodies in a place where people can come. I don't know why.

There is not much connection between a saint's consciousness and the body that he has left. There is oftentimes a much better connection with a young mureed who has never seen the saint or the body. And this running back to the burial place is not contributing too much to our development towards balance, though it is very popular nowadays. It is a looking back into the past, a long past expression of a teacher that you have come beyond.

When I was in India, I visited Inayat's burial place for only one reason: I knew that everyone would ask me when I came back if I had visited it. Only for that reason. It is not through the place that one contacts him. It is just like going to some rock where people know where a great saint has been, or you go to a place on the beach where he has left his footsteps and touch them, or you have a photograph. Remember the story of Inayat Khan giving me his photograph? The moment when he sensed my reaction is a great example of balance. For he realized at once that there was something else that I should do.

There is not one path that everyone should follow. Everyone has his specific path, and everyone should be following that or finding out what it is, for that is what will bring him fastest into a state of balance.

This is why you can't ask another, even some "great master", to tell you what you should do.

Jelaluddin: Balance always emanates from the inner planes, and not from external authority, be it a "master" or anything?

Shamcher: Right. Exactly! As Buddha says in his farewell address: "Look to the Light within yourself, look at no other person or teacher or connection outside of yourself!"

Jelaluddin: Speaking of Buddha, what is the "middle path"?

Shamcher: That is the path of balance.

Jelaluddin: The Sufi path is supposed to be the path of direct experience. To me this means the acquiring of a sense of presence: the presence of God within you, the presence of God coming through your teachers within you, an awareness of the presence of your soul.

Shamcher: When you use the word "God" you have to be careful. For instance, many so called great mystics say, "God told me this from the other side." So whenever they hear a voice from the other side it's God? Well, what kind of God is that?! Sometimes it is a very immature spirit that is trying to get back to this world because this is the only one he understands, and so he will come back to anyone that will listen. These people who are always going around saying that they are in direct contact with God are not the real mystics. What an inadequate expression of God!

Jelaluddin: Perhaps they have made a "god" of the object of their obsessive desire.

Shamcher: Yes! That's why even the word "god" can be misused and is misused. I saw an advertisement in the newspaper once of someone who said, "I talk to God". Well, isn't that wonderful, I thought, so do I.

Jelaluddin: Superstition, Shamcher, I see as a craving for a higher sense of order significance in one's life. And I see it arising after a long period of time where one has lacked that kind of meaning and sense of higher significance. So when one suddenly gets a glimpse one seizes on it and says, "Yes, this is explaining my whole life."

Shamcher: This is what I would call the high form of superstition. The low form is when one has all types of negative interference, and thoughts that tomorrow the world is going to end and you're going to go to hell.

It is a positive sort of superstition when you feel the urge to expand because you think that you have found a solution to everything. You may get caught up in this, but usually after a while you finally see that you don't really know it yet, and then finally you come to the point to where you say, "Well, I don't know it yet, but it doesn't matter, I am beginning." And this is beautiful because you are listening now instead of making assumptions. From that point on you have no superstitions anymore, or at least not serious ones.

A very common form of this superstition is when people read about karma and reincarnation. "Oh yes, now I understand everything!" But each of us understands the concepts of karma and reincarnation in a different way. Inayat Khan was very careful to explain - in a sense explain away - the ideas of reincarnation and karma to us. He said that what most people think of reincarnation is not you, not yourself that was reincarnating, but the mind stuff. Look at Buddha, His whole life was to try and get us away from the idea of karma and reincarnation, so we would not have to be born again here.

Jelaluddin: Is the Soul subject to states of obsession?

Shamcher: No. The Soul is supreme and is always as it is. It is only that the Soul forgets itself in the mind that is subject to superstition or obsession. Of course very few people really live in the Soul or remember the Soul.

Jelaluddin: Shamcher, Inayat Khan stressed moderation in the undertaking of spiritual disciplines, didn't he?

Shamcher: Yes, I could give you an example of what he meant from my worldly experience.

In the dunes near Oceano in California there lived a man who was an abstract painter. He was a recluse and his occupation very well fitted his life. He lived about a mile from me, and whenever I would come walking past he would say, "O, Bryn, Bryn, come in." And then he would talk for an hour without interruption because he hadn't mastered the art of being alone and was rather desperate for company. He had exaggerated to himself his ability to live in solitude and now he had to have these outlets. He talked and talked and he would even say things like, "You know that Moon Mullins next door is running up and down the beach stealing all my lumber." It wasn't his lumber of course. This shows his unbalance. And the danger of being alone when you are not really capable of it. So many do this. Run up to the Himalayas or something.

I almost succumbed to this in 1959. I was in the Himalayas and I found myself walking up along a streamlet. The water was fresh and fresher the higher I went, and it was so beautiful and easy that I did even feel myself moving after awhile. And I began to think that this was the place that I should spend the rest of my life. Then, just as I was thinking this, I saw a cave, you know, one of those caves where you'd expect a saint to be looking out from the opening. So I said to myself, "Oh, this is exactly where I should stay, but how am I to get in?" And then I discovered by climbing higher that there was a way of getting in.

It was really dark. And as I was feeling around I felt something soft that went GRRR-GRRRRR, and then I felt again and it went GRRRRWHHAHHHHHHHWHAHHH and I got out of there.

Later on I looked at this bear, for that's what it was I think, as something pushed by Inayat Khan to tell me to get out of there and get out in world again. So I went back to the world and began once again to fight for OTEC (Ocean Thermal Energy Conversion.)

Before this, you see, I had been fighting rather in vain for OTEC,

47

and had an experience where I was talking to Prime Minister Nehru and a room full of scientists, where I felt that they were listening, and were interested, but that nothing would come of it so I might just as well go on retreat.

But then I got thrown out of that cave. And before I knew it, all of America was talking OTEC, and I was in the middle of it, so there were some very good reasons why I couldn't just sit in solitude.

Jelaluddin: Didn't a yogi once tell Pir Vilayat that the holy men in the Himalayas were a dying race because the way for us now is to stay in the world?

Shamcher: Yes. They are a dying race because the world is now ripe to take care of itself. It doesn't need saints sitting back there keeping us in touch. And this is coming! You see young people everywhere, and many old people too, who have become aware of the need for balance in the spiritual realities, of the need for a balance that will make them much more than simply the heirs of religious traditions.

One time the Dalai Lama said that a certain Trappist monk was the only person from the West that he knew of that could meditate, but you see it coming among all the young people around us now, so there is a direct contact with what I would call the stream of the universe among them or at least some of them.

Jelaluddin: I understand that Inayat Khan talked about a sort of progression among the Spiritual masters and that since the time of Mohammed, the message that he completed, there is no longer any necessity to use a go-between for enlightenment.

Shamcher: Yes. Except that when you say the word "master"- Inayat Khan never used that expression about any human being. And he was the first to say that he was not a master. He would always say, "There is only one master, the spirit of guidance, that leads every soul to its destination." So I become offended when I hear people talk of Inayat as a "master", of course, though he may have

48

been in a sense the greatest one for us. I really don't like this word "master".

Jelaluddin: What is the spiritual path?

Shamcher: If one would be facetious one would say that there is no such thing. But if one is kind, and accepts it, one would say that in the line of Inayat Khan, it is annihilation of the false ego.

This annihilation of the false ego is much different and bigger task than is usually realized. For some it may take a million years. Others may seem almost as if they are born with it. Some people work really hard at it and never seem to succeed, and then they've apparently got it, until the next day when they haven't got it anymore!

You know, humans are so crazy sometimes they really succeed! The funny thing is, many times it is the less you try, the better you do. All life is for this purpose, whether one calls it a spiritual path or not. The difference between the other paths and what we call the "spiritual" path is that the spiritual path has an element of knowing and conscious seeking. But then again, for some people, it may not be such a good thing to be conscious of it.

Jelaluddin: So what's the point of joining any spiritual path or order?

Shamcher: So why join an order if you feel like that?

Jelaluddin: No Shamcher, I'm only asking a question.

Shamcher: There is every point and no point at all. The person who doesn't join may be every bit as wise. One follows an impulse, and that impulse is the best one can do at the time.

I know people who are, in a sense, more conversant with Sufi attitudes and ways than many of the Sufis, yet who would find it a horror to join the group. Others join, of course, and are very successful because they join, so there is no attempt at a general rule here. I myself have always been in doubt about groups: "Should I

49

join or should I perhaps not join?" And after I have joined: "Should I stay in or get out?"

It doesn't really matter! But sometimes I have felt like I was cheating the people who were not in the group but were trying so hard to get in, while I who was in the group wasn't really sure that I wanted to be there. So was perhaps giving the wrong impression. But then I would decide that to leave would be wrong against all the people who were still in who would wonder, "Why does he leave us now?"

Jelaluddin: It sometimes can be really frightening to have only God and yourself to depend on.

Shamcher: Personally I don't see any difference. I am very happy alone, and I have often felt that I joined with Inayat Khan not to receive comfort from him but for what I could contribute to his movement. Not that he personally needed anything.

One time Inayat was approached by a man who said that he liked his message very much but that he couldn't join the organization because he had to be free. And Inayat answered him, "Well, I think I am free and yet I am in the organization, but I don't think you are so free because you are afraid of organizations."

So if you are afraid to join or not to join, you are not free. If you join as a matter of your own free will, join with the thought that you are doing so because you want to help its cause. Because if you join with the idea that it is going to give you comfort you may be extremely disappointed, because it may not give you comfort. You shouldn't want anything from the organization. About this you shouldn't care.

Jelaluddin: But you think it's all right not to join and just to depend on your own being?

Shamcher: Yes. It is quite all right just to depend on your own being. God, to me at least, is all the comfort one ever needs, and more. And I don't take comfort from anyone else.

Made in the USA
Las Vegas, NV
29 January 2022